Triumph over Tragedy

Triumph over Tragedy

Donna Anthony

XULON PRESS

Xulon Press
2301 Lucien Way #415
Maitland, FL 32751
407.339.4217
www.xulonpress.com

Paperback ISBN-13: 978-1-6628-3823-1
Ebook ISBN-13: 978-1-6628-3824-8

Table of Contents

Acknowledgements

I am grateful to God for His faithfulness. He has been my Rock in every situation in my life. Father, thank You for never leaving me or forsaking me. I love You.

James, my love, my friend, my husband, I love you forever. Thank you for believing in me and pushing me to defy fear by stepping into dimensions of my purpose. I am grateful to share this journey with you.

To my Megan, I love you. You are one of God's greatest gifts and assignments in my life. You also pushed me to defy fear and step into dimensions of my purpose. Mommy loves you beyond words.

I want to honor my parents Willie and Genevia Gathings (deceased) for making me the woman I am today. I thank my parents for loving me unconditional and instilling in me to be the best version of myself. I miss you guys so much, and I hope I have made you guys proud.

To my sister, Theresa and her family, my immediate/extended family, and Pleasant Ridge House of

Worship church family, thank you for loving me and believing in me.

Minister Jacqueline McMath, I am so thankful for you being that prophetic voice in my life. You have spoken so many things into my life that has come to pass, and book writing is one of them. Keep allowing God to use your voice as His mouthpiece.

Apostle/Bishop Anthony Hatcher, thank you for speaking into my life in October 2018 about writing books. What was spoken over my life in 2018 is now coming to pass. Thank you

LaPortia Binder at BinderKaptures Photography, I want to thank you for the beautiful photos. Your patience and professionalism were one of a kind. You made this experience memorable.

Greg Dixon and the editorial staff, I am so thankful for your help with this book. Your careful eye and attention to detail are a tremendous gift. Thank you for everything you do to support the calling on my life.

Logan Mungo and the Salem Publishing team, thank you for your guidance, excellence, and genuine desire to see others flourish. Thank you for making my dream a reality.

Introduction

*W*hat do you do when it seems as if your world is caving in and there's nothing you can do or say to stop it? The situation is truly out of your control, and you feel helpless, hopeless, and afraid all at the same time. Well, that is what happened to me on March 18, 1997. That is the day my world turned upside down.

On that dreadful day, March 18, 1997, I lost my mom, Genevia Fears Gathings, suddenly and unexpectedly. We had just celebrated my twenty-fourth birthday, and we had had a great time laughing, grilling, and just having fun with the family. Mom was there having fun and laughing like we normally did. Although she suffered from asthma, she was not sick and did not complain about having any issues that day or the months leading up to it. So, when I got the call from my father, I could not believe what I was hearing on the other end of the phone. I was not prepared mentally, emotionally, spiritually, or physically for this untimely news. I was blindsided, devasted, and felt like giving up. Mom was a beautiful, vibrant, funny, loving, caring, compassionate, and devoted mother and wife who loved God and loved life. In my finite mind, I thought she had at least another forty-plus years to live. I thought she would help me raise my daughter and watch her grow up and have kids one day. Boy, was I wrong?

On that day, my dad called around 5:30 pm and said as calmly as he could that something was wrong with Mom and that my sister and I needed to come up as soon as possible. I remember asking him what was wrong with her and dad saying, "Bae, I believe Mom is dead. So, you and your sister need to get here quickly." My heart immediately sank, and I fell to the floor with my four-month-old daughter in my arms in disbelief. I do not even remember how I got dressed to go to Dad's. My husband was not home at the time, so I really felt like I was going to lose it. I have never felt so helpless in my life. Tears flowed down my cheeks while I sat holding my daughter, Megan. My sister called crying and asked if my husband James was home so we could all go together, but I told her that he had not made it home yet. I was not in a good place where I would be able to drive myself, so my sister and her husband picked me and Megan up, and we traveled to Dad's house. That was a long, dreadful trip. I was praying that when we got there, we would see that he had made a mistake. Maybe she had just fainted and was not dead. I was wrong again.

When we arrived at the house, we were met with cars parked everywhere, and I knew then that something was indeed wrong. The coroner was in the house, and Mom was still lying on the floor. I remember running inside and being met by my crying grandmother, and then my dad came from the back bedroom and hugged my sister and me. I wanted to see Mom to make sure that it was her, because I was still in denial. When I went in the bedroom, I saw that it was her, and she looked like she had been trying to call someone. I remember feeling the coldness and stiffness of her body as I laid upon her crying. I had never felt pain like that before.

My mother's death hit me extremely hard because she was my world, my everything. Beside God and because of the uniqueness of pregnancy, my mom was the first person who knew me, loved me, cared for me, felt me move and kick, and held me. That is why her untimely, sudden, unexpected death was an enormous shock. It literally felt as if a part of me died that day. My heart was broken in a million pieces, my emotions were all over the place, and my will was screaming, "Give up, Donna!" Even though I knew giving up was not an option, I didn't feel like I had the power to fight.

Growing up, I had always said that I didn't know what I would do if my mother, father, or sister died because we were a very close-knit family. My mother, sister and I would do everything together, especially since Dad worked the night shift. My mom worked in the school system, so she was always home with my sister and me. She would drop us off at school in the mornings and pick us up in the evenings. We were often mistaken as sisters instead of mother/daughters, so when she died, my world was turned upside down. I had experienced pain, hurt, and loss before her death. However, the pain from losing her was colossal and on a whole other level. It was so overwhelming that for many days, I did not know whether I was coming or going.

A Life-Changing Event

*M*y mother's death was a major life-altering experience for my family and me and the most difficult thing I have ever experienced. It seemed like everything in my life changed. I never fathomed the depth of pain, loneliness, hopelessness, and helplessness a person experiences from losing a mother until it happened to me. I have always had compassion for others who had lost their mom but did not understand the depth of their pain. I realized that at times, life can throw you a curveball that you are not ready to catch. There is not an owner's manual to prepare you for this.

I was only twenty-four years old when my mother died. I had been married for only two years and had just given birth to a beautiful four-month-old girl, so the timing of her death just seemed wrong to me. Even though, I knew that I was not in control of the timing of her death, it just seemed unfair. To me, this should not be happening at this point in my life. This was supposed to be the time when Mom started enjoying life

1

since retirement, traveling more, shopping more with my sister and me, and loving on her grandkids, Michael, and Megan.

As a matter of fact, my family, my sister and her family, and Mom and Dad had started vacationing together and just living life. She often talked about how she was going to spoil her grandkids. Boy, that dream was short-lived, and out of nowhere, like a thief in the night, she was no longer with us. I had pictured her helping me raise Megan and being around for every one of Megan's special events. I never thought she would be just a memory and not here guiding me along the journey of marriage and motherhood. She was the epitome of a God-fearing wife and mother. After her death, I relied on those memories to guide me. I often think how proud she would have been to see my sister and I patterning our life after hers. I did not realize how precious life is and how quickly it can be taken away from you until my mom died. The void of a loved one can leave you feeling empty.

One of the first words I remember asking my sister after Mom's death was, "Where is the owner manual that explains how to cope with the death of your mom?" I asked Dad how we were going to make it through this. The only thing he said was, "It is going to be alright, daughter. God does not put no more on you than you can bear." At that moment, I felt like it was more than I could handle. I got really mad at him for saying that because he was trying to be positive, and I was still looking at the situation in a negative sense. My sister was trying to be strong for me. The only things she said was, "Donna, we got each other and God, and we are going to be just fine. Sis, Mom would want us to keep living our life." I did not doubt that, but I did not want to hear that. I finally came into agreement with them, because they were not hearing my negativity.

Even though my dad and sister portrayed a positive attitude around me, I still worried about how they were coping with mom's death when I wasn't around. I wondered how Dad was going to make it since he and Mom had been married so long. I did not want him to give up on life and then my sister and I would be parentless. I also wanted to make sure my sister was going to be alright. I really believe that a person does not learn how to cope with grief until it happens to them. I can truly say that I did not learn how to cope with Mom's death until it happened in my life, and even then, it has been a process—one that only God and time can heal, and where I am learning how to trust Him for my continued healing. At times, I did not know how I would make it through the day. But God!

Oftentimes, we do not like to think about the reality that one day our mom, dad, siblings, grandparents, etc. are going to die, and when it happens, it will feel like time has stopped. It seems unbelievable, unimaginable, and unthinkable that your loved one will not be around any longer. I wondered how in the world I would make it day by day if I were to lose a parent, sibling, or someone else very close to me. Well, that dreadful day happened, and there were many days I did not think I was going to survive, but God gave me the grace that empowered me to keep walking and put one foot in front of the other.

Emotional Distress
I Experienced

*I*n addition to being devasted, I also experienced so many emotions, ranging from feeling guilty to sad, all in a matter of twenty-four hours. I felt guilty because Megan and I had headed to Mom's house to pick her up, because she wanted to be there when Megan got her ears pierced. I felt like if I had been there, maybe I could have stopped her death. The only reason I turned around and went back home was because it looked like it was about to storm, and I did not want to get caught in it. That took place around 11:00 am.

At that time, I called Mom to let her know that I was going to wait to get Megan's ears pierced because it looked like a storm was brewing, but the call didn't go through. Instead, I got a busy signal. The phone stayed busy from that moment until when Dad called. I thought that was strange, but I figured maybe Mom had forgotten to hang the phone up completely after talking to me. It never occurred to me that something might have happened to her because I had just spoken with her, and she was so excited to go get Megan's ears pierced. Guilt tried to consume me, because I felt like I had let her down. I had to realize that her death was out of my control. This was her appointed time, and it was going to happen whether I was there or not. As a matter of fact, Job 14:5 comforted my heart. It says, "Man's days are determined; you have decreed the number of his months and have set limits he cannot exceed" (NIV). I knew that mom's days on earth were determined, and there was nothing I could have done to prevent her death from happening. I had to release the guilt to God because I knew He cared for me. That scripture along with many, many more was what I hung around my neck to reassure me.

I also experienced times of shock, numbness, and denial. I did not know until I started taking classes on death and grief that I was experiencing normal stages of grief. I learned that there are five stages of grief: denial, anger, bargaining, depression, and acceptance. These five stages are considered a universal framework of what a person may experience during grieving. I wish I had known this earlier because it would have helped me better understand what I was experiencing instead of thinking something was wrong with me.

As I compared my experience with the five stages of grief, my initial response to mom's death was shock. I did not realize that shock was my body's way of protecting itself from nervous system overload until reality set in. After shock, I was overwhelmed with a sense of denial.

I really did not believe that my mother, my best friend, the one who loved me unconditionally would no longer be physically present with me, no longer be able to give me advice and encourage me. It just did not seem real. I thought I could just compartmentalize what had happened and deal with it later, but guess what? I was wrong. I had to deal with my mother's death and face the reality that she was gone, and I would never see or hear her again on this side of heaven. When I say that was a hard pill to swallow, it truly was. I had to face reality so my sister and I could help Dad make funeral arrangements.

I had to force myself to deal with every emotion and the loss of my mother, my hero and best friend. There were many days that I felt loss and no sense of direction. During those times, I found myself praying and reading the Bible more, especially when I could not talk to my dad, my sister, or my husband. I believe God was using those times to draw me closer to Him. Even though I was saved, I needed a closer relationship with the Lord, and boy, this was the experience that spearheaded it. I wanted God to tell me that I was dreaming, but instead He told me through His Word that His grace was sufficient and that in my weakness, His strength would be made perfect (2 Corinthians 12:9). Once I heard that, I knew that Christ's strength was going to help me through this experience.

Reality Sets In

*T*he reality of my mom's death was extremely difficult for my family and me to accept. My mother was the epitome of a mom, wife, aunt, sister, daughter, and friend. She touched so many lives, especially since she worked in the school system for years. I kept believing that I would wake up from the extremely difficult experience, and Mom would call me or drop by to visit. For days, I did not have an appetite and could not sleep. All I wanted to do was sit in a corner and think about what I could have done differently that day. So many thoughts and emotions would plague my day that it was starting to interfere with my daily routine.

The day arrived for my father, my sister, and I to visit the funeral home to make funeral arrangements. Boy, that was extremely hard. My dad and sister were still trying to hold it together for me, but I could see in their eyes the tears they were trying to keep from falling and could tell that they were hurting just as bad as I was. We talked with the funeral director of Carter's Funeral Home in

West Point, Mississippi, who was nice and understanding. She really tried to make our experience less painful. We discussed what we wanted and how we wanted Mom's funeral service to flow. After we gave her the information and pictures, she took us to the room where the caskets were. Oh my, I did not think I was going to make it. My knees begin to shake, my voice began to tremble, and the tears begin to flow. It was as if a river of stored tears were released. The funeral home director gave us some time alone to process what was happening. I remember Dad giving my sister and me a big bear hug and telling us that everything would be alright. He said, "Donna, you got to get yourself together before you make yourself sick." My sister was trying to hold it together as much as she could and said, "Come on, Donna, we can do this. We got God and each other to lean on."

After I released the tears, we were able to pick out a beautiful pink casket. We finalized everything, and the director told Dad to bring back everything they needed to make Mom look just as beautiful as she was. Mom's visitation was scheduled for the following Friday, and her funeral was that Saturday. When I left the funeral home, I could not see how everything was going to be alright. The only thing I was feeling was a pulsating, achy, nagging pain in my innermost being.

I vaguely remember the funeral, because I guess a part of me was still in denial mode. I blocked a lot of it out because to me, this was the finale. I would never see her face again. She would never be around to help me with my daughter or to pray with me, talk to me, or give me advice when I had a problem. She made my worst days my best days and always had a prayer, an answer, and, most importantly her love. Do not get me wrong, our dad was phenomenal. He was always in our corner. However, when Mom died, he went to another level in his care for his children and grandkids. God really groomed our father to take on multiple roles in our lives. His grandkids became the light at the end of the tunnel of his pain. He channeled all his energy into making sure his grandkids, my sister, and me were taken care of emotionally, mentally, and physically. Like I said earlier, we were a very close-knit family. Even though Dad was hurting and in pain, his main concern was making sure his girls and their families were good.

Mom's death forced me to grow up and build a closer relationship with God because that was the only way I was going to make it through this pain. Even though I had Dad and my sister, I had to trust God to heal my heart. I had to realize that the reality of talking with, praying with, and seeking advice from Mom was over and had to accept what was and trust God for what would be. I knew that one day this pain would eventually ease, I would heal, and the memories of her would live on in my heart daily. The watery eyes and the lingering pain lasted for a while, but God.

A Lingering Pain and Watery Eyes

I came to realize that there is a no clear-cut time-table for grieving. It is truly a process. I remember going through some dark days for weeks when I could not sleep or eat. I did not want to talk to anyone or go anywhere. All I wanted to do was sit in a corner and cry. Even though I had a four-month-old daughter who I love dearly and means the world to me, I found it difficult at times to care for her and perform household chores. My husband could not motivate me to get up and get moving. It was like I just did not have the energy to do anything that I wanted to. Even though I had the love of my husband, father, sister, and an awesome brother-in-law, none of them could take away the gut-wrenching pain that I felt deep within my soul.

I remember my husband saying to me after a few weeks of me not being myself, "Donna, you are going to the doctor." He felt like maybe the doctor could give me something temporarily to help me rest and sleep. Sure enough, James took me to the doctor while my sister babysat our daughter. I told the doctor what had happened through tears and what I was experiencing as far as not being able to eat, sleep, or rest—that I did not want to be around anyone or go anywhere. The doctor felt like I was dealing with anxiety and depression, so he prescribed me some medicine to help as well as some medicine for sleep. I took the medicine off and on for about two weeks but did not like how it made me feel. It made me feel weird and out of touch. I knew that taking those meds would not work, because I needed to be alert to take care of Megan since James had gone back to work. I finally came to the point where I knew I would have to stop taking the medicines so I could be fully alert to care for a four-month-old baby.

As I continued reading the Bible, I began to read scriptures on healing and how God is the same God of yesterday, today, and forever (Hebrew 13:8). I knew from reading the Bible that God indeed healed then, and I knew that if I had faith to believe God for my healing now, it would happen. I'm not saying that God does not heal through medicine because He does, but the medicine was not working for me in regard to how I was feeling. I also believe that God wanted to heal my soul from the gut-wrenching pain I had experienced since day one of mom's death. I knew that He was the only One who could heal my soul pain.

I can remember like it was yesterday. After about two weeks, I put Megan down in her crib for naptime. I got in my favorite spot on the floor next to our bedroom window and begin to pray and ask God to take away this pain so I could function and fulfill my duties as a mother, wife, sister, coworker, etc. I asked God to heal me from the inside out so I could be whole and help someone else along the way. I told Him I was tired of feeling helpless, hopeless, and worthless. And out of nowhere, I heard a small voice say, "Get up, daughter, and live because your daughter needs you." I looked around the room to make sure James had not come home, because I knew Megan was sleep and could not talk like that. The audible voice said those words again, "Get up, daughter, and live; your daughter needs you."

It dawned on me that the voice was the Lord pulling me up from the pit I had fallen in. I knew that He was trying to get my attention because life goes on. Without a doubt, God was answering my prayers and showing me that He cared for me and loved me unconditionally. I realized that this was my breakout moment. My daughter needed her mommy to be whole and healed so I could parent her like I was supposed to. I had been so consumed with the pain of losing my mom that I was forgetting about the gift God had blessed James and I with.

I looked at Megan sleeping in her crib and said, "Baby girl, Momma is getting up to live again." At that moment, I got up off the floor, got the medicines, and threw them in the garbage. I stepped out in faith and began to declare life out of my mouth. I declared that I would not be depressed, that I would not take any more pills for depression and anxiety, and that I would live and not die. It was as if what I had read in the Bible was coming back to me. In Proverbs 18:21, the Bible says that life and death are in the power of the tongue. I chose life.

I also made a confession to the Lord that when He healed me completely, I would surrender my life totally to Him. I knew without a doubt that I was being healed on the inside. It seemed like the moment I made my confession followed by my action, the Lord healed me and gave me a new life. I knew that my mom would not want me to live like I had been but would want me to get up, take care of Megan, be the wife that I could to my husband, be the daughter to look after dad, be the sister to be there for my sister, be the granddaughter to be there for my mom's parents, and be the aunt to my niece and nephew.

Although I missed her, I learned how to live and enjoy life again. Mom's memories will forever be a part of my life, and I can carry them everywhere I go. I also learned that faith is something that must be put into action. My faith in God grew to new heights, and I began to trust God and surrender my life to the One who gave me life. God healed my soul from the gut-wrenching pain. He healed me from anxiety, depression, hopelessness, helplessness, and worthlessness and gave me a new outlook on life. He began to do amazing things in my life all because I stepped out in faith.

One Year Later

*A*s my relationship with God grew, my faith increased. I knew that no matter what I or my family faced going forward, the Lord was by our side. Deuteronomy 31:6 (NIV) says, "Be strong and courageous. Do not be afraid or terrified because of them, for the LORD your God goes with you; he will never leave you nor forsake you." I memorized this scripture and declared it every time I felt weak or afraid. I realized that in the past, my relationship with God had been shallow. Even though I had been baptized at the age of seven and both attended and served at church faithfully, my relationship with God did not go deep. I knew of Him, but when Mom died, I begin to experience His love, compassion, care, and faithfulness on a personal level.

One year later, on February 21, 1998, God gave me a spiritual overhaul, and I really begin to see that even in the midst of losing my mom, God is still God, and that God can bring about something good to your life in the midst of tragedy. The good for me was a closer walk with

Him, a new spiritual identity that had been covered up by all the pain I was experiencing. I realized that I could still have joy, peace, and laughter and be happy again. This spiritual overhaul made me seek God more, pray more, and read my Bible more. The more I read the Bible, the more hopeful I became, and my faith began to grow. The biblical scripture of Romans 8:28 (NIV) became a cornerstone scripture for me: "And we know that in all things God works for the good of those who love him, who have been called according to his purpose."

As I began to study the Bible more, there were several other verses that became cornerstone scriptures for me as well. First Thessalonians 4:13-17 ignited a fire of hope and revelation on the inside me. It gave me hope and joy to know that one day I would see Mom again if I stayed connected to the Lord. I began to look at death through a different lens and began to see it not as the end but as a new beginning with a new body living in a new place. I began to have a new pep in my step, and a few years later, I even shared this passage at my grandpa's funeral.

My Grieving Process

*G*rieving is a process, and everyone grieves differently. After taking a class on grief, I learned that
grieving is the make-up of a person's emotional state,
the circumstances surrounding the death, the relationship with the deceased, the person's support system,
and their natural coping mechanism. I also learned that
some people may feel better after a few weeks or months,
while others may take years. The grieving process can
be painful, grueling, and very lonely because during the
healing process, you may experience setbacks and draw-
backs. Because of this, it is very important that people
who have lost someone give themselves time to allow
the process to unfold.

Grieving may vary as a person navigates through
the healing process. During the grieving process, I felt
like I was on an emotional roller coaster. I learned that
you have to go through every hurdle, bump, and valley
without judging yourself because each experience is
moving you forward and will work out in the end. God

knows what we need, and He knows when to give it to us. I just had to learn how to trust Him through that difficult time. I knew that eventually I would experience victory over this emotional experience if I kept trusting God because the Bible declares, "But thanks be to God who gives us the victory through our Lord Jesus Christ" (1 Corinthians. 15:57).

Everyone's experience with grief is different. For me, it was an experience that shook me to my core. As mentioned earlier, I had only been married for about two and a half years and had a four-month-old daughter. I was still adjusting to being a wife and a new mother. I had always leaned on my mother for advice, especially when I did not understand something or needed to know how to cook a certain dish or just needed someone to talk with and pray with.

As I reflect on the Sunday before mom's death, I remembered mom being so full of life and energy. She seemed normal to me when she and my dad visited us that Sunday. She wasn't sick, and her asthma was under control. However, two days later, she was gone. That was hard to wrap my head around because Mom was my biggest cheerleader and the epitome of unconditional love. She would put other people's needs before her own. She even babysat Megan when I worked the 5:00 am shift. She did not mind getting up early. That was just the type of person she was, there to help whenever.

I did not realize how much my mom was the center of my world until she died. She had such a large presence in my life, it's no wonder that her death left a huge void. I had to learn how to move forward. Even though everyone's story and process are different, the two things that are the same for everyone is the void and not seeing their loved one around every day. These two things can cause unexplainable emotional pain. If I had to grade my emotional pain on a scale with one being no pain and ten being intense pain, I would give myself a ten plus for about the first several weeks. It eased a little after the funeral, but it was still high for the first few months. When I went back to work, my pain was not as bad because I was focused on my work and talking to other people. But when I would get off work and start the trip home, I would cry a lot. Then when I picked Megan up from daycare and made it home to do housework, it would ease, maybe because I was focusing on her and cooking dinner. The moment I would sit down to relax, my emotions would start going crazy again. When I was alone, they were at their worst.

Holidays, birthdays, and special occasions were dreadful and very difficult for me for the first few years because they were a reminder that Mom was no longer with us. My parents had a way of making every holiday memorable—Mom with her famous turkey and dressing and my father with his famous greens. Even though Dad was amazing and tried to fill in the void after Mom's death, her presence was greatly missed. We had to make many adjustments that first year. My father became the holiday planner and cook and would make sure that everything went well. I finally learned how to cook cornbread dressing, yams, greens, and potato salad.

My family had to create new traditions, and this helped us move forward together. My dad gave my sister and I certain dishes to cook for special holidays. He had many shoes to fill now: family planner, dad, granddad, adviser, listener, and family go-to person, and he walked in all of them with amazing grace. This made special holidays less grievous for us, and we begin to laugh and have fun again. Our dad played a major role in helping create new memories while not allowing Mom's memory to fade.

Years Later

*D*ays turned into weeks, weeks turned into months, and months turned into years. I am always reminded how much I miss her but am thankful to those who were there for us and allowed us to lean on them during this time. There were days when I just wanted to pull the blinds, stay in bed, and crumble, letting myself cry for a while because of the pain I was experiencing. Crying helped me release emotions that were pent up inside of me. I realized that how I was feeling was affecting my home life, but my husband was so supportive. He gave me my space to grieve while trying to encourage me. After those first few months, the pain lessened, and I was on the road to restoration. God was restoring my joy, laughter, peace, and my life once again. I had to accept what had happened to move forward and trust God in and through the process. Years later, I am still trusting God to continue to walk with me on this journey.

My Journey to Healing

As I began to heal, I wanted to share my experience with anyone who would listen to me because I realized that that was part of my healing as well. I wanted to share my experience in writing in order to help others who were struggling with the death of their mom or any other loved one. In this way, writing became part of my therapy.

After going back to work after my mom's death, I would come across people who had lost their mom and were still struggling with it. I believe those were opportunities God was giving me to share my experience and that if the Lord could heal me and give me a new lease on life, He could do the same for someone else. Telling others about my experience became my outlet. God put me in so many situations where my testimony became something others could lean on. I shared my ups and downs with them because I knew that being transparent was the only way healing could continue in my life and the only way healing could start in theirs.

I released my feeling with the stroke of a pen. Dr. James Pennebaker, author of *Writing to Heal: A Guided Journal for Recovering from Traumatic and Emotional Upheaval,* explains that stress often occurs from emotional obstruction. He also explains that when a person can began to write about his or her experience, the experience can then become graspable (as cited in Pennebaker, 2004). Susan Zimmermann, author of *Writing to Heal the Soul: Transforming Grief and Loss Through Writing,* explains that the simple act of putting down your deepest thoughts and feelings on paper is one of the most powerful and effective means to ease and ultimately heal sorrow (as cited in Zimmermann, 2002). Writing helped me bring structure and order to the chaos of grieving and allowed me to tap into the healing power of my unconscious. Writing also allowed me to give voice to my fears and despair while allowing self-healing to invade my space. Writing truly became an effective and powerful means of working toward a better, healthier me.

Exercise also became part of my healing therapy. I took a likening to yoga, going to the gym, and taking short walks. The more I incorporated exercise into my daily life, the better I felt. I begin to feel vibrant and alive again. The more I moved, the more I wanted to move. It was as if God had given me a new talk, a new walk, and a new zeal to live.

Even though I missed Mom, I decided not to allow her death to affect me in a negative way, but rather to cherish the memories in my heart and live. I knew deep inside my soul that this is what she would want me to do.

One scripture that I quoted a lot during this process and still quote today is Romans 8:28, "And we know that all things work together for good to them that love God to them who are called according to his purpose." I knew that eventually God would work everything out for my good and for His glory and that through this experience, I would help others.

Meditation was another part of my journey and helped bring a sense of peace into my life. Starting each day with prayer and meditation became a source of power and allowed me to talk to God and listen to His instructions. I learned how to pray the Word of God during this time, because I realized that God's Word was the spiritual food, I needed to heal the pain inside.

My hope and faith in God grew stronger, as well as my determination to live and build a stronger relationship with God. It was during my prayer and meditation time that I knew that no matter what happened in life, God was in control and by my side and had a greater purpose and plan for my life. Even though my sister, my dad, and I had suffered a great loss, God gave us the strength to move forward and live.

Self-care became a part of my healing therapy as well. Self-care was important so I could keep thriving, healing, and living life. When I needed a reboot, I would spend a day at the spa getting a manicure, pedicure, and a massage. I absolutely fell in love with massages. They became a stress reliever for me. Facials were also stress relievers for me since I would get occasional breakouts due to stress. Spa therapy was a central piece to recharging and rebooting my mind, soul, and body and a way I could focus solely on myself while Megan was at daycare. Even today, I still practice self-care, prayer and meditation, exercise, and writing as part of my continued healing regiment.

Having a good support system played a crucial role in my healing. My husband was great after the initial day of my mom's death. He took some time off work when she first died to make sure that I was alright. Whenever I needed to talk, a hug, or someone to be there while I shed some tears, he was there for me.

My father, my sister, and my brother-in-law were also a part of my support system, even though they were hurting themselves. My sister was trying to be strong for me, and my dad was trying to be strong for my sister and me. He was great, even though I know that during his quiet times, it was tough on him. But he didn't let that stop him from being a present help in both of our lives. He became the grandparent who loved his grandkids unconditionally. I am so grateful for how they supported me during this difficult time in my life.

My mom's family was also part of my support system. They would call and check on my sister and me. My grandma would call just about every day! She wanted to make sure that we were well. Aunt Mary became like a second mom to my sister and me. They really tried to help us navigate through this difficult time.

My boss, Kimberley, was very supportive during this time. She came to the funeral along with other co-workers and that was very uplifting to me. My co-workers were there to lift me up when I went back to work, and they gave me space to grieve. I really appreciate them for that.

My former pastor was another huge support. He would call and check on me and my family and always had an encouraging word to say. He would pray with me and give me hope through God's Word that everything would be alright. He really steered me closer to the Lord during this difficult time. I know that if it were not for the grace of the Lord, I could not have made it through. The Lord used my pastor to show me the importance of having a relationship with Him. He was a great inspiration in my moving forward.

MOVING FORWARD

*T*he one thing that I realized while going through the death of my mother was that life is precious and we should enjoy every day loving on each other. I remember reading in the Bible that life is like a vapor that appears for a little time and then it vanishes (James 4:14 NIV). That statement is so true. I also realized that the pain eases over time. I had to adapt to a new way of living life without Mom. As days, weeks, months, and years went by, my mom's death was no longer a constant in my mind. I was finally able to start moving forward because her memories would forever live in my heart, and the soul bond we shared would forever be a part of my life.

As time went by, my thoughts about Mom were happy thoughts and not sad, dreadful ones. With the progression of time, my heart did not feel so broken and torn into a million pieces, and I had peace that could only come from my relationship with the Lord. I had to choose to allow the Lord to do a new thing in my mind, emotions, and will. I had to choose to learn to not allow my mom's death to affect me in a negative way. Apostle Paul said it like this in Philippians 3:13-14 (KJV), "Brethren, I count not myself to have apprehended: but this one thing I do, forgetting those things which are behind, and reaching forth unto those things which are before, I press toward the mark for the prize of the high calling of God in Christ Jesus." I had to press toward my healing so that I could be the best momma to Megan and the best wife to James.

My primary focus became my relationship with the Lord, my daughter, my husband, and my family. I had to wake up and snap out of the miry clay of sadness, gloom, and not wanting to move forward and start living life again. I had to learn the power of living in the now, become aware of my thoughts, and no longer identify with my pain. One particular verse became a staple point for my thought life: Proverbs 23:7 (KJV), "For as he thinketh in his heart, so is he." I had to choose to think positive, happy, joyous thoughts and not sad, depressed thoughts. I realized that my thoughts were the battlefield of the enemy, and I had to begin to cast down every thought that was not of God and choose not to allow mental chatter to be the vehicle that drove my emotions and mind. As I became more aware of my thoughts, I begin to see a major shift in my emotions.

Regaining and building emotional strength through positive thoughts helped me to accept the things I could not change and move forward experiencing happiness and joy again. I was finally getting Donna back. I had to come to the realization that my life had changed and adjust accordingly. It was like God was taking me through a transformational period of letting go and starting afresh with Mom's memories in my heart. I was eager to smile, live, and laugh again and move forward in this new normal of being the best Christian, mom, wife, sister, and daughter that I could be. My good days began to outweigh the bad ones, and I learned not to complain but to enjoy life. I was opening myself up to loving life again in a new way.

Final Thoughts

$\mathcal{R}$ecovering from the death of my mother was not easy. There were a lot of things I did not understand about death and grief. Even though, I had lost a very close cousin, the pain was different when Mom died. I felt as though I was never going to recover from this, but God had other plans. He knew that eventually I would overcome the pain and help others who had lost loved ones.

This recovery period was met with a lot of emotional challenges. I learned a lot about myself and who God was to me. My relationship with Him grew and flourished from this difficult process, and I learned that no matter what happens in my life, God is always there by my side, and He will never leave me nor forsake me. Even when I felt alone, I knew deep within my soul that God was there working everything out for my good and for His glory. Yes, even the death of my mother was going to work for God's glory and my good. The good that came out of Mom's death was a deeper and closer relationship with God. My purpose was birthed from my pain, and I know now that I am walking in my purpose. Jeremiah 29:11

says, "For I know the thoughts that I think toward you saith the Lord, thoughts of peace, and not of evil, to give, you an expected end." These words became scripted on my heart, and even today, I trust the plan and purpose of God for my life. I do not always understand the process, but I trust Him. I have learned to walk by faith and not by sight, even when I can only see a part of God's plan. God does not give us the full blueprint for our lives, because He wants us to trust Him and walk by faith.

The death of my mother birthed a new beginning for me in my Christian walk. I had an urgency to study God's Word every chance I got. My prayer life grew, and my relationship with God became stronger than ever. I had a hunger and thirst to witness to others about my experience, and how God had delivered me out of the miry clay of sadness that was so deep. God was working something good in me that would later be instrumental to so many people. Who would have thought that out of the miry clay of sadness, hopelessness, and sorrow would emerge a young preacher woman who is a lover of God and the gospel of Jesus Christ! I pray that my life experience of the death of my mother, my best friend, my confidant will help someone else who is struggling with the loss of their loved one.

Message from the Author

I know that the death of a mother is not an easy life experience. Your life is changed in so many ways. But you must choose to live or else you will drown in the sorrow of your pain. For me, after months of feeling stuck in the miry clay of despair and hopelessness, I made a choice to live again and to enjoy life. Has every day been a walk in the sun? No, but I choose to look at each day as a new day of growth from the pain of losing her. My prayer is that anyone who is dealing with the loss of your mom or any other loved one will find peace, comfort, love, and consolation in the days, weeks, and months to come after reading this book. Learn how to be patient and easy with yourself and the process of healing. Practice self-care and reach out for therapy if you need it. Make sure to surround yourself with caring, loving, heart-centered, and understanding people. Do not be afraid to release your loved one and move forward, because the reality of the matter is that their memories will live forever in your heart. Above all, I pray that everyone reading this book will be healed from the inside and that healing will radiate on the outside.

Summary

*T*his book is written from a heart of love and compassion to help someone who is struggling with the loss of a mother, father, sister, brother, or any other loved one. It is a journey into my life when I lost my mother to a sudden death and what I learned through the process. I hope that through my experience, you will find hope, support, comfort, and peace as you navigate through your own grieving process.

References

Pennebaker, James W. 2004. *Writing to heal: a guided journal for recovering from trauma & emotional upheaval.* Oakland, CA: New Harbinger Publications.

Zimmermann, Susan. 2002. *Writing to heal the soul: transforming grief and loss through writing.* New York: Three Rivers Press. eBook.